What Do I See When I Stop To Look?

Written by Sarah Coulter

Illustrated by Anna Lindgren

Psalm 19:1-4 NIV

The heavens proclaim the glory of God;

the skies proclaim the work of his hands.

Day after day they pour forth speech;

night after night they reveal knowledge.

They have no speech, they use no words;

no sound is heard from them.

Yet their voice goes out into all the earth,

their words to the ends of the world.

Hello, Fellow Explorer!

There is a world of mystery and awesomeness awaiting you, and it is just out your front door. Grab a notebook, a pencil, and a camera. As we stop to look, we will meet new friends that will tell us a bit about the world around us. I invite you to linger as you observe each friend. As you pause and reflect, you will find that each friend reveals a deeper Biblical truth, emboldening you to know a very special Friend.

Let's Go!

What do I see when I stop to look?

An American toad hiding cautiously by a stone.

--> 2 Corinthians 10:4 NLT

"We use God's mighty weapons, not worldly weapons, to knock down the strongholds of human reasoning and to destroy false arguments."

American Toad lays her eggs at her water source. The eggs are laid in long strands that sit a few inches below the water's surface. At first glance, they may look quite vulnerable, but these eggs sport a silent and mighty weapon. The eggs are counter-shaded, meaning they are darker on top and lighter on the bottom. This unique coloring knocks down the strongholds of the predator's reasoning. The eggs are not noticed, no matter if the predator is looking down into the dark depths of the water or looking up toward the light of day.

What do I see when I stop to look?

A Familiar Bluet damselfly pausing momentarily on a reed.

GALATIANS 2:20 NLT

"My old self has been crucified with Christ. It is no longer I who live, but Christ lives in me."

Familiar Bluet Damselfly started out as a swimmer, no wings at all. Slight changes took place over time as he grew. During one of his final stages, wing buds grew in. It was then that he knew it was time to swim to land and climb the tall grasses. As he paused on a large blade of grass, his skin-like skeleton cracked open along his back and head. Emergence! He crawled out of his old skin and emerged as a new creature- a damselfly!

What do I see when I stop to look?

A longhorn band-wing grasshopper jumping sporadically through the air.

ACTS 4:31 NLT

"After this prayer, the meeting place shook, and they were all filled with the Holy Spirit. Then they preached the word of God with boldness."

Grasshoppers have an exoskeleton, which simply means their skeleton is on the outside. As they grow, it gets cramped, and they have to shed their skeleton. This is called molting. Usually, the grasshopper will molt five to six times before reaching adulthood. To shed his skin, Longhorn Band-wing Grasshopper swallows air. Gulp. Gulp. He fills with air until the exoskeleton cracks. On the final molt, Longhorn Band-winged Grasshopper emerges with a new boldness. He now can move and jump even better, and soon he'll be able to fly.

What do I see when I stop to look?

A Calico Pennant dragonfly buzzing hurriedly over the pond.

MARK 1:35 NIV

"Very early in the morning, while it was still dark, Jesus got up, left the house and went off to a solitary place, where he prayed."

You may have noticed that dragonflies are impressive flyers. Zip. Whizz. Zoom. Up, down, left, right. Calico Pennant Dragonfly's movements remind us of a helicopter. He is also quick, zooming at speeds comparable to an ATV. It is interesting to note that each morning before all this impressive high energy can take place, Calico Pennant Dragonfly must pause. This moment of solitude allows his wings to warm up. Once his warm-up has taken place, there is no stopping him!

What do I see when I stop to look?

A short-winged green grasshopper camouflaging secretly in the grass.

> PSALM 31:19, 20 NLT

"How great is the goodness you have stored up for those who fear you. You lavish it on those who come to you for protection, blessing them before the watching world. You hide them in the shelter of your presence safe from those who conspire against them. You shelter them in your presence, far from accusing tongues."

Mother grasshopper is equipped to keep her eggs safe. Finding the perfect spot to lay her eggs, she uses two flaps at the end of her stomach to dig down in the sand. Once her abdomen is deep below the surface, she lays her eggs underground. Mother Short-winged Green Grasshopper won't stay to care for the young, but they will remain safe, sheltered until they hatch.

What do I see when I stop to look?

A Southern leopard frog burrowing deeply among the leaves.

PSALM 16:1 NIV

"Keep me safe, my God,
for in you I take refuge."

Often Southern Leopard Frog sits along the edge of the pond, but when he senses danger, he seeks refuge. Jumping into the pond, he takes one sharp turn then surfaces among the plants at the water's edge. He is safe, resting securely.

What do I see when I stop to look?

Blazing Star standing stunningly beside the boulder.

INVITATION TO
FAITH Conversation

PHILIPPIANS 2:2 NLT

"Then make me truly happy by agreeing wholeheartedly with each other, loving one another, and working together with one mind and purpose."

Blazing Star is easily spotted from a distance. The purple flowering stalks of this plant can stand two to three feet tall. And while it appears that Blazing Star is calling attention to itself, a closer look reveals something remarkable. Tiny blooms, which open up from top to bottom, work together to create each one of the brilliant spires.

What do I see when I stop to look?

A pink-spotted ladybird beetle cruising hungrily among the foliage.

→ JOSHUA 23:9-11 NLT

"For the LORD has driven out great and powerful nations for you, and no one has yet been able to defeat you. Each one of you will put to flight a thousand of the enemy, for the LORD your God fights for you, just as he has promised. So be very careful to love the LORD your God."

While she may be out and about right now, Pink-spotted Ladybird Beetle loves to visit the vegetable gardens in town. This small beetle fights a tough battle for the gardener as it gorges itself on aphids, an enemy of the vegetable garden. Pink-spotted Ladybird Beetle can eat up to 60 aphids a day. She strategically lays her eggs next to clusters of aphids so they can move in on the prey as soon as they hatch. The gardener will take special care to protect this visitor.

What do YOU see when YOU stop to look?

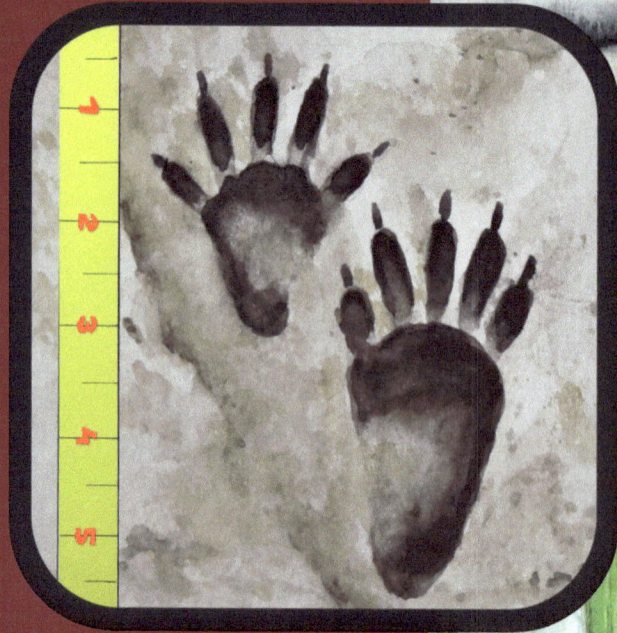

INVITATION TO
FAITH Conversation

JOSHUA 4:6-7a NLT

"We will use these stones to build a memorial. In the future, your children will ask you, 'What do these stones mean?' Then you can tell them..."

Tracks are found along the pond's edge. They remain to tell a story. Something transpired while you were away. The tracks remind you that you are not always present for everything that is happening, that there is a world bigger than the one you see day to day. The tracks await your attention. They entice you to ask the question, *What do these mean?* They want to teach you about the world you live in and the God who created it.

How to Identify

1 First, you need something to identify. Taking pictures while on a walk is a great way to keep that creature close to you while trying to figure out its proper name.

2 Once you have a picture of a creature that you want to identify, you have to make a choice of what resource you're going to use. You may choose to use the internet or maybe a field guide. A field guide is probably a better starting point.

3 After that, start with the basic identification. Usually, field guides are organized by the type of creature you're trying to identify: dragonfly or frog, turtle or cricket.

4 Next, you'll have to look at identifying characteristics, which vary. Sometimes you look at the markings, other times you may have to look at the shape of the wing or head. Just remember that it takes time. If you don't find it in one book, you may have to look in another. It's fun to learn different names while you look. And even if it's not the name of the creature you're trying to identify now, you may see it later.

5 Don't just go by the picture. Read the descriptions also to be sure that you have identified it correctly. When you find the description that most closely matches the creature that you have, you probably have got the right one. However, as you continue your study, you may gather other clues to the identification of that creature that causes you to question your original conclusion.

6 Don't be afraid to reevaluate and have fun!

The short-winged green grasshopper gave me a lot of trouble. I couldn't find one that looked anything like him in the resources I was using. Part of the problem was that (and I found this out as I was doing my research) grasshoppers are often identified by their wings. He was not flying in the picture I took, so his wings were not showing. Eventually, I was able to identify him by the slant of his head. It took forever!

The longhorn band-wing grasshopper gave me similar problems. I eventually found a picture that looked exactly like him and I was like "That's it!" Then, I read the description for the "Carolina Grasshopper" and found out they didn't live in Tennessee. I knew I had to continue my search.

At first, I thought the damselfly was an Eastern Forktail, but then I realized that, when resting, his wings didn't touch his body. The wings of an Eastern Forktail do touch the body plus the "Eastern" Forktail is found in Wisconsin!! Therefore he was most closely identified as a Familiar Bluet damselfly, which has lifted wings and actually lives in Tennessee.

I learned that some toads can be identified by the markings on their bellies. Unfortunately, I didn't know that before taking my toad's picture. He was first mistaken for a Southern toad but the name which I thought referred to all of the south, actually refers to the southwest.

Troublemakers

Meet the Author & Illustrator

Sarah Coulter and her husband Todd are both educators living in the land of Texas. At this time Sarah is at home with her two kiddos, Ameilia and Lucason. She enjoys getting them outside to escape the noise and busy-ness of life to explore God's natural playground. Sarah hopes that this book will nudge others to do the same. She encourages her readers to revel in the finding of a hidden spider web or new seedlings growing in the sandbox. Sarah believes that noticing these things and talking about them will help each one involved in the experience to better know our Creator.

Anna Lindgren resides in Grand Rapids with her husband Luke and son Magnus. She finds inspiration in nature on their family walks and enjoys harvesting wild edibles and collecting beach rocks on beautiful Lake Michigan. She is dedicated to sharing her art, creating murals, custom art and book illustrations. Anna has spent years teaching art in hopes to inspire others to discover the passion of making beautiful things because, "It's worth making everyday a little extra beautiful!" More of her art can be viewed at www.annasartavenue.com

www.ingramcontent.com/pod-product-compliance
Lightning Source LLC
Chambersburg PA
CBHW041547260326
41914CB00016B/1577

* 9 7 8 1 7 3 4 0 8 9 1 0 3 *